P9-DEK-486

LOVE YOURSELF

Like Your Life Depends On It

by

Kamal Ravikant

Copyright © 2012 Kamal Ravikant

All rights reserved. This book or any portion thereof may not
be reproduced or used in any manner whatsoever without the
express written permission of the publisher except for the use
of brief quotations in a book review.

ISBN–13: 978–1478121732
ISBN–10: 1478121734

Cover design by Sajid Umerji
Book design & layout by Perseus Design

Printed in the United States of America

To James, Kristine, and Sajid.

You made this book happen. Thank you.

Contents

Foreword

In December of 2011, I was invited to be a participant at Renaissance Weekend in Charleston, NC. Not what you think — no jousting knights or fair maidens. Instead, a conference attended by CEOs from Silicon Valley and New York, Hollywood types from LA, and politicians and their staff from DC. It's like TED, but everyone is assigned to participate in panels or give a talk. The application asked for awards won and recognitions received, and as an example, listed the Nobel Prize. Really.

I have no awards to speak of. Or pedigree. No Goldman Sachs or Morgan Stanley on my business card. When the founder of the event introduced me to the audience at a talk I gave — the title assigned to me, "If I could do anything..." — he said, "Kamal cannot keep still. Whether as an infantry soldier in the US Army or climbing the Himalayas or walking across Spain on an ancient pilgrimage, he's always moving." He'd done his research. I don't remember the rest, but I remember his last line, "I'm sure he'll have something interesting to share with us."

I had exactly two minutes to stand on a podium and address an audience of scientists, Pentagon officials, politicians, and CEOs — all far more qualified than I to talk about pretty much anything. The speaker before me had been the youngest person to graduate from MIT. Full honors, of course. Before him, the youngest Thiel fellow.

It's interesting what goes through your mind at moments like these. Time slows down, yes. But that's almost cliché. There's only the podium and the microphone. You step up. The audience grows blurry, as if out of focus. Clock starts.

And then I knew what to do. I would offer something no one else could. My truth. Something I'd learned purely from my experience, something that saved me. The audience came into focus.

"If I could do anything," I said into the microphone, "I would share the secret of life with the world." Laughter from the audience. "And I just figured it out a few months ago."

For the next two minutes, I spoke about the previous summer, when I'd been very sick, practically on bedrest. The company I'd started nearly three years ago was struggling, I'd just gone through a breakup, and a friend I loved suddenly died. "To say I was depressed," I told them, "would have been a good day."

I told them about the night I was up late, surfing Facebook, looking at photos of my friend who'd passed, and I was crying, miserable, missing her. I told them about waking up the next morning, unwilling to take it anymore, the vow I made, and how it changed everything. Within days I started to get better. Physically, emotionally. But what surprised me

2

was that life got better on its own. Within a month, my life had transformed. The only constant being the vow I'd made to myself and how I kept it.

Afterwards, and for the rest of the conference, people came up individually and told me how much what I'd shared meant to them. One woman told me that sitting in the audience, listening to me, she'd realized that this was the reason she came. All I'd done was share a truth I learned.

A month later, a friend was going through a difficult time, so I quickly wrote up what I'd learned that summer and sent it to him. It helped him a lot. Months after, I shared it in an email with James Altucher, a friend and my favorite blogger. He replied, offering to feature it as a guest post on his blog.

Naturally, I refused.

Truth be told, I panicked. Lots of my friends read his blog. I'm an entrepreneur in Silicon Valley; it's fine to write about startups. But this stuff?

"You have to share this," James wrote back. "It's more important than 'here's how to be an entrepreneur' or 'here's how to bulk up in 30 days.' This is the only message that's important."

I shared my fear with him — what would people think? His response, something that I will never forget and will always be grateful for: "I don't do a post now unless I'm worried about what people will think about me."

So I struck a deal with him. I'd kept notes about what I'd learned, the practice, how I'd succeeded and failed. I would put those together in a book and send it to him. If he liked it, I'd publish it.

And that's how we ended up here.

What is this about?

Loving yourself. Same thing your mom told you, same thing self—help books repeat enough times to be cliché. But there is a difference. It's not lip service. It's not a fire and forget type approach. It's something I learned from within myself, something I believe saved me. And more than that, the way I set about to do it. Most of it, simple enough to be idiotic. But in simplicity lies truth. In simplicity lies power.

Starting with the writeup I sent to my friend, this is a collection of thoughts on what I learned, what worked, what didn't. Where I succeed and importantly, where I fail daily.

As a wise friend likes to remind me, this is a practice. You don't go to the gym once and consider yourself done. Same here. Meditation is a practice. Working out is a practice. Loving yourself, perhaps the most important of all, is a practice.

The truth is to love yourself with the same intensity you would use to pull yourself up if you were hanging off a cliff with your fingers. As if your life depended upon it. Once you get going, it's not hard to do. Just takes commitment and I'll share how I did it.

It's been transformative for me. I know it will be transformative for you as well.

Beginning

I was in a bad way. Miserable out of my mind. There were days when I'd lie in bed, the drapes closed, day outside sliding into night and back to day, and I just didn't want to deal. Deal with my thoughts. Deal with being sick. Deal with heartache. Deal with my company tanking. Deal....with....life.

Here is what saved me.

I'd reached my breaking point. I remember it well. I couldn't take it anymore. I was done. Done with all of this. This misery, this pain, this angst, this being me. I was sick of it, done.

Done. Done. Done.

And in that desperation, I climbed out of bed, staggered over to my desk, opened my notebook, and wrote:

"This day, I vow to myself to love myself, to treat myself as someone I love truly and deeply — in my thoughts, my actions, the choices I make, the experiences I have, each moment I am conscious, I make the decision I LOVE MYSELF."

There was nothing left to say. How long it took me to write this, less than a minute perhaps. But the intensity, it felt like

I was carving words onto paper, through the desk. I'd been disgusted with myself — I could love another and wish them well, but what about me? From now on, I would focus only on this thought. For me.

How to love myself, I did not know. All I knew was that I'd made a vow — something far greater than a commitment, bigger than an I—wish or a nice—to—have. A vow. I was going all in or destroy myself trying. There was no middle ground.

In my bedroom, in the darkness, with a city outside that had no idea of the decision that'd been made or even cared, I set out to love myself.

And the way I did it, it was the simplest thing I could think of and one that I knew I was capable of. I started telling myself, "I love myself." A thought I would repeat again and again. First, lying in bed for hours, repeating to myself, "I love myself, I love myself, I love myself, I love myself, I love myself...."

The mind would wander, of course, head down rat holes, but each time I noticed, I'd return to repeating "I love myself, I love myself, I love myself, I love myself...." and it continued.

First in bed, then showering, then when online, then when I'd be talking to someone, inside my head, I'd be going, "I love myself, I love myself, I love myself, I love myself." It became the anchor, the one true thing.

And I got better. My body started healing faster. My state of mind grew lighter. But the thing I never expected or imagined, life got better. But not just better, things happened that were fantastically out of my reach, things I couldn't have dreamt of. It was as if life said, "Finally, you idiot! And let me show you that you made the right decision."

It did. People came into my life, opportunities arose, I found myself using the word "magic" to describe what was happening.

And through it all, I kept repeating to myself, "I love myself, I love myself, I love myself, I love myself."

In less than a month, I was healthy, I was fit again, I was naturally happy, I was smiling. Amazing people were coming into my life, situations were naturally resolving themselves. And through it all, whether I was at my computer again, or kissing a pretty woman, in my head, I'd be telling myself, I love myself.

In all honesty, in the beginning, I didn't believe that I loved myself. How many of us do? But it didn't matter what I believed. All that mattered was doing it and I did it the simplest way I could think, by focusing on one thought again and again and again and again until it was more on my mind than not.

Imagine that. Imagine the feeling of catching yourself loving yourself without trying. It's like catching a sunset out of the corner of your eye. It will stop you.

Why love?

Why not "I like myself?" Or, "I accept myself?" Why oh why oh why does it have to be love?

Here's my theory: If you've ever been a baby, you've experienced love. The mind knows it on a fundamental, even primal level. So, unlike most words, "love" has the ability to slip past the conscious and into the subconscious, where magic happens.

What if you don't believe that you love yourself? Doesn't matter. Your role is to lay down the pathways, brick upon brick, reinforce the connections between the neurons. The mind already has a strong wiring for love. The body knows it as well. It knows that love nurtures, that love is gentle, that love is accepting. It knows that love heals.

Your job is not to do any of these. Your job is purely to love yourself. Truly and deeply. Feel it. Again and again. Make it your single-minded focus. The mind and body will respond automatically. They don't have a choice.

Here's the best part, one that makes me smile as I write this. As you love yourself, life loves you back. I don't think it has a choice either. I can't explain how it works, but I know it to be true.

When you find yourself using the word "magical" to describe your life, you'll know what I'm talking about.

The practice

I've tried to break down exactly what I did that worked. And how one can replicate it. Comes down to three things which I'll explain in later chapters:

1. Mental loop

2. A meditation

3. One question

All three gently return me to self—love. That's the beauty of this practice. It's simple, it's practical, and the results are far greater than you could imagine.

After all, if you loved yourself truly and deeply, would you limit your life to what you previously thought possible? Nope. You'd blow your own socks off.

There is one requirement. A fierce commitment to loving yourself. This, I'm afraid, can't be skipped. What if you don't believe that you love or, heck, even like yourself? Doesn't matter. If you have to build up to it, that's ok. The practice works in a way the mind is designed to function. The mind has no choice but to adapt and respond.

Just remain open to the possibility of loving yourself. The rest is easy.

Window

Darkness is the absence of light. If you remember this, it will change your life. Changed mine. It is this concept that the practice is based on.

Any negative thought is darkness. How do you remove it? Do you fight fear or worry? Do you push or drown away sadness and pain? Doesn't work.

Instead, imagine you're in a dark room and it's bright outside. Your job is to go to the window, pull out a rag, and start cleaning. Just clean. And soon enough, light enters naturally, taking the darkness away.

It's that simple. Each time the mind shifts to darkness — fear, worry, pain, you name it — when you notice, clean the window. Light will flow in.

Mental loop

I sit at my desk. San Francisco sparkles through the large bedroom windows. A Coca Cola sign blinks off, then rebuilds itself, one letter at a time. I see cars on Market street, red taillights. The famous tower over twin peaks is swallowed up by the night, hidden by fog.

A neighbor's balcony light comes on. Sliding door opens, a woman in shorts and t—shirt steps out, kneels to pick something up, then returns inside. The door shuts.

If you were to open up my head at this moment and peer within, you'd find yourself asking with a thick Southern drawl, "Does this boy not have an imagination?"

There is only one thought running through my head: I love myself. I love myself. I love myself.

For days, ever since I made the vow, this has been my only focus. Sometimes as a whisper, sometimes silent. When I brush my teeth, mumbling. In the shower, loud. Non—stop. I love myself, I love myself, I love myself.

I have nothing to lose. This is all there is. I love myself, I love myself, I don't give a damn about anything else, I love myself.

I once heard someone explain thoughts as this: we, as human beings, think that we're thinking. Not true. Most of the time, we're remembering. We're re–living memories. We're running familiar patterns and loops in our head. For happiness, for procrastination, for sadness. Fears, hopes, dreams, desires. We have loops for everything.

We keep replaying the loops and they in turn, trigger feelings. It's automatic to the point where we believe that we have no choice. But that is far from the truth.

Imagine a thought loop as this: a pathway laid down by constant use. Like a groove in rock created by water. Enough time, enough intensity, and you've got a river.

If you had a thought once, it has no power over you. Repeat it again and again, especially with emotional intensity, feeling it, and over time, you're creating the grooves, the mental river. Then it controls you.

And that is why a focused mental loop is the solution. Take this one thought, I love myself. Add emotional intensity if you can – it deepens the groove faster than anything. Feel the thought. Run it again and again. Feel it. Run it. Whether you believe it or not doesn't matter, just focus on this one thought. Make it your truth.

The goal here is to create a groove deeper than the ones laid down over the years – the ones that create disempowering feelings. They took time as well. Some we've had since childhood.

Which is why this requires a focused commitment. Why it must be a practice. Forget demolishing the grooves of the past. What you're creating is a new groove so deep, so powerful, that your thoughts will automatically flow down this one.

It takes time, sure. Took me a month to go from misery to magic. But you will notice changes, shifts in your feelings, beautiful happenings in your life. Expect them. There'll be more and more until one day, you'll be walking outside in the sunshine, feeling good, loving life and life loving you back, and you'll stop and realize that it's now your natural state.

Can you imagine a better way to be?

A meditation

Even if you don't do anything else, please do this. It will make a difference.

Each day, I meditate for seven minutes. Why seven minutes? Because I put on a piece of music that I like, one that is soothing and calm, piano and flute, one that I associate good feelings with, and it happens to be seven minutes long.

I sit with my back against a wall, put on my headphones, listen to the music, and imagine galaxies and stars and the Universe above, and I imagine all the light from space flowing into my head and down into my body, going wherever it needs to go.

I breathe slowly, naturally. As I inhale, I think, I love myself. Then I exhale and let out whatever the response in my mind and body is, whether there is one or not. That's it. Simple.

Inhale: I love myself.

Exhale: Breathe out what comes up.

Inhale, exhale, inhale, exhale. Natural. The music flows.

The mind wanders, that's its nature. Each time it does, I just notice where I am in the breath. If inhaling, I shift to I love myself. If exhaling, I shift to letting out whatever is in the mind and body.

Occasionally, I shift my attention to the light flowing in from above. Sometimes, I do that each time I inhale.

Before I know it, the seven minutes are up and the meditation is over.

There is something to this, the thought of light flowing into my head from galaxies and stars. The concept of light itself. Just like love, the subconscious has a positive association with light. Plants grow towards the light. As human beings, we crave light. We find sunrises and sunsets and a bright moon beautiful and calming.

Once again, there's no need to consciously create healing or anything positive. The subconscious takes care of it. All I have to do is give it the image − in this case, light; give it the thought − in this case, loving myself. It does the rest.

This is an intense practice because it is focused. But does it feel intense? No, quite peaceful, actually. I think that's what real emotional intensity is, one that creates peace and love and growth.

Instructions

Step 1: Put on music. Something soothing, gentle, preferably instrumental. A piece you have positive associations with.

Step 2: Sit with back against wall or window. Cross legs or stretch them out, whatever feels natural.

Step 3: Close eyes. Smile slowly. Imagine a beam of light pouring into your head from above.

Step 4: Breathe in, say to yourself in your mind, I love myself. Slowly. Be gentle with yourself.

Step 5: Breathe out and along with it, anything that arises. Any thoughts, emotions, feelings, memories, fears, hopes, desires. Or nothing. Breathe it out. No judgment, no attachment to anything. Be kind to yourself.

Step 6: Repeat 4 and 5 until the music ends.

(When your attention wanders, notice it and smile. Smile at it as if it's a child doing what a child does. And with that smile, return to your breath. Step 4, step 5. Mind wanders, notice, smile kindly, return to step 4, step 5).

Step 7: When music ends, open your eyes slowly. Smile. Do it from the inside out. This is your time. This is purely yours.

Why music? Since I listen to the same piece each time, it now acts as an anchor, easily pulling me into a meditative state. A crutch perhaps, but a nice one.

Do this meditation consistently. You will notice the magic that occurs.

One question

It's easy to say "I love myself" while locked inside my apartment, recovering from being sick. Tougher when I'm back to the land of the living, interacting with people who have their own issues and mental loops.

That is where the question came from. In dealing with others and reacting to their negative emotions with my own, I found myself asking this question:

If I loved myself truly and deeply, would I let myself experience this?

The answer, always, was a no.

It worked beautifully. Because I'd been working on the mental loop, the step after "no" was clear. Rather than solving the emotion or trying not to feel it, I would just return to the one true thing in my head, "I love myself, I love myself, I love myself."

This question is deceptively simple in its power. It gently shifts your focus from wherever you are — whether it's anger or pain or fear, any form of darkness — to where you want to be. And that is love. You mind and life have no choice but to follow.

I'm in love

"You're so pretty," I say.

She walks alongside my friend, Gabe, holding his hand. Her dark hair freshly cut, layers. Cool February night in the mission district in San Francisco. We're heading for tacos.

Her smile doesn't change. She doesn't say thank you, the way a woman would to a genuine compliment. Instead, she says, "I'm in love."

We pause to cross the street.

"It's true," she says, "that's why. I'm in love."

She's pretty regardless, but I get what she's talking about. She glows. Non-stop smile. Full of life.

When I get home, before I go inside, I pause and realize something. The love, it doesn't have to necessarily be for another, does it? Love is an emotion, love is a feeling, love is a way of being. That spring in the step, that smile, that openness, can't it simply come from loving ourselves?

That stops me. Of course. Here we are, thinking that one needs to be in love with another to shine, to feel free and shout from the rooftops, but the most important person, the most important relationship we'll ever have is waiting, is craving to be loved truly and deeply.

And here's the interesting part. When we love ourselves, we naturally shine, we are naturally beautiful. And that draws others to us. Before we know it, they're loving us and it's up to us to choose who to share our love with.

Beautiful irony. Fall in love with yourself. Let your love express itself and the world will beat a path to your door to fall in love with you.

Another meditation

This one, I'm a little scared to share. People will think I've lost it. But it is powerful.

Step 1: Set a timer for 5 minutes.

Step 2: Stand in front of a mirror, nose a few inches away. Relax. Breathe.

Step 3: Look into your eyes. Helps if you focus on one. Your left eye. Don't panic, it's only you. Relax. Breathe slowly, naturally, until you develop a rhythm.

Step 4: Looking into your left eye, say, "I love myself." Whether you believe it that moment or not isn't important. What's important is you saying it to yourself, looking into your eyes, where there is no escape from the truth. And ultimately, the truth is loving yourself.

Step 5: Repeat "I love myself" gently, pausing occasionally to watch your eyes.

When the five minutes are up, smile. You've just communicated the truth to yourself in a deep, visceral way. In a way the mind cannot escape.

If anyone ever looked in your eyes, knowing that you loved them, this is what they saw. Give yourself the same gift.

Love and memory

Memory is not set in stone. Any neuroscientist will tell you that. The more you remember something, especially if it's emotionally charged, the more you will reinforce the pathways connecting the neurons. Simply put, the more you think about it, the more you feel it, the stronger the memory.

Here's the interesting part. It's not just the act of recall that strengthens a memory, another factor shapes and even changes it — the state of mind you are in when remembering something.

The implications of this are transformative.

Take a random experience, a relationship that ended years ago. Consciously recall it when you're miserable. You'll naturally find yourself focusing on the negative parts, and those will grow stronger in memory.

Conversely, same exact experience, but recall when you're happy. Notice the change?

It's still the same experience, it's still your mind. But the filter is different. And the filter shifts the focus, which subtly changes the memory. More importantly, it changes how the memory makes you feel, the power it has over you.

There's a solution here, a powerful one.

If a painful memory arises, don't fight it or try to push it away — you're in quicksand. Struggle reinforces pain. Instead, go to love. Love for yourself. Feel it. If you have to fake it, fine. It'll become real eventually. Feel the love for yourself as the memory ebbs and flows. That will take the power away.

And, even more importantly, it will shift the wiring of the memory. Do it again and again. Love. Re—wire. Love. Re—wire. It's your mind. You can do whatever you want.

Change

"It's happening,"

"Yes."

"Really happening."

I nod slowly, grin.

"Unbelievable," she says. "Unbelievable."

Through the window, the Sierras below, mountains of earthy brown. Daybreak ahead. A clear morning. This high up, no human could survive, yet we hurtle forward at hundreds of knots in an aluminum tube, comfy in our chairs, sipping our sodas.

"Are you sca—" She rests her hand gently on my arm. "Nervous?"

I look out for a moment, the land below already flattening, then to her. "Nope."

"I don't know how you can do that. Me, I'm a bucket of nerves."

"But this is magic," I say. "Why be nervous, that's not doing any good."

"I know that," she says. "I do, really. But tell that to my nerves."

"I think," I say, "I think that I'm starting to accept the magic, that life can be this way, that fantastic experiences, things I couldn't imagine within my reach are possible, are happening, will happen. That's what it is."

She smiles, squeezes my arm, then leans into my shoulder. She closes her eyes. I reach down and kiss her head softly, smelling her hair, then return to the window.

Patchwork of browns and greens below. How fast the land's changed. How fast everything changes.

Light switches

Richard Bandler, co—founder of NLP, got known early in his career as someone who could cure schizophrenics within hours. He started getting called by doctors and patients' families to go to mental institutions, work with the worst cases, the ones everyone had given up on.

One of his favorite stories is about an executive who started hallucinating snakes. No one could convince him otherwise. He was committed, received treatment, no luck. So, he was strapped to his bed — not very empowering when you believe snakes are crawling all over you — in the mental hospital and chalked off as one of the incurable ones.

By the time Bandler met him, he was in bad shape. To figure out what to do, Bandler went for a walk in town. He needed to snap this guy back to reality. He passed a pet store and noticed a barrel full of rubber snakes on the curb. He went inside, asked the man behind the counter if he could rent the entire barrel for a few hours.

"They're for sale," the man said. "I don't rent the whole barrel."

"I need them," Bandler said, "all. But only for a few hours."

"Why?"

"I'm going to cure schizophrenia," Bandler said.

"Cool," the man said.

Bandler chalks it up to the fact that since the store owner wasn't a doctor, his mind was open to cures that were out of the norm. Turns out he also had a few well–trained snakes – two cobras and one giant python that loved wrapping herself around humans. Perfect.

The store owner and Bandler returned to the mental hospital, bags full of rubber snakes and three real ones, went to the shower where the patient bathed, and covered the place with them. The live cobras, he put extra close to where the patient would be. The python, right above where he'd position the wheelchair. Finished, he surveyed his work.

It reminded him of the scene from Raiders of the Lost Ark where Indiana Jones descends into a chamber full of writhing snakes. Enough to scare anyone, let alone a person with heightened snake phobia.

Keep in mind, Bandler once cured a guy who thought he was Jesus by bringing in three muscular football players dressed as Roman Centurions and wood for a life–size cross into his hospital room. Then, he proceeded to nail the cross together, pausing occasionally to measure the guy as the Centurions held him down. By the time they were ready for the crucifixion, the man was convinced he wasn't Jesus. Even after the drama had passed, the cure stuck.

The snake owner and doctor stood behind the one–way glass to the shower. Bandler brought the man in, strapped tight in his wheelchair. The moment the man saw the snakes, he started screaming, "Snakes!" It was a terrible sound, Bandler says, from the very depths of the man, carrying throughout the hospital, "Snaaaaaakes!" But he positioned the man right where he could see the cobras in front and the python dangling above. Then he left and shut the door behind him.

The man screamed and screamed. Bandler waited. Finally, he went in. The man saw him, was about to scream, but Bandler cut him off.

"Snakes snakes, yes I know," Bandler said. "Tell me which ones are real and which ones aren't, and I'll wheel you out. Otherwise, I'm leaving you in here." Then he turned to go.

"Rubber snakes," the man said, motioning to the ground with his head. "Hallucinated snakes," he motioned around. Then, eyes up at the python dangling a few feet above, dropping closer, "real snake!"

This caught Bandler off guard. The man, when put to the test, was not only lucid enough to distinguish real from hallucinated, he could even tell which ones were rubber – something even

Bandler had a hard time telling, given how realistic they were.

He wheeled the man out and asked him how he could tell hallucinated versus real.

"Easy," the man said, "hallucinated snakes are see—through."

The man had known all along. Reality was solid, hallucinations were see—through. But his fear was so intense, he'd lost touch with reality. Bandler taught the man to focus on the difference between reality and hallucinated see—through snakes and the man was cured. He still saw hallucinated snakes occasionally, but knew that they were not real. The power they had over him was gone.

Fighting fear doesn't work. It just drags us in closer. One has to focus on what is real. On the truth. When in darkness, don't fight it. You can't win. Just find the nearest switch, turn on the light.

James Altucher, in one of his best blog posts, talks about how he stops negative thoughts in their tracks with a simple mind trick. "Not useful," he tells himself. It's a switch, a breaker of sorts, shifts the pattern of the fear.

In the last book of the Hunger Games trilogy, one of the main characters has been tortured by the Capitol, his memories altered so that he can't distinguish between actual and implanted memories. His friends come up with a simple exercise. They tell him memories they know to be true, then ask, "real or not real?" Slowly, he learns to distinguish real from not–real until his mind adapts and he realizes that not–real memories have a certain shininess to them. And when in doubt, he returns to the practice: real or not–real.

Fear, when used properly, is a useful tool. It serves us well when near a blazing inferno or standing at the edge of a cliff. But outside of this, it's hijacked the mind. To the point where it's difficult to distinguish the mind and our thoughts from fear itself.

So, these tools, like light switches, exist. When fear arises, remember that it is a hallucinated snake or that it's not useful or that it's not real. All three work. There's many more, ones we can come up with ourselves, if we wish. As long as it works, it's valid.

Key is this, when in darkness, have a light switch you've chosen standing by. For example, in writing this book, fear says that I'm risking what people will think of me. Doesn't matter. My role is to recognize it for what it is — hallucinated snake, not useful, not real — and continue on.

Coasting

As I write this, I'm probably the lowest I've been in a while. Things are just....so. Not as bad as they were when I first started, but life's not zinging. The thing is, when life just works for a while, you get used to it and you think it'll stay that way. Recency bias. When things suck, when you're deep in it, it seems like they will suck forever. You can't imagine a way out. When things are great, you live as if it'll always last.

So, I ask myself, if I was to look deeper, why am I down, why isn't my life an expression of, well, awesomeness? Once you've experienced it and you know it's possible, then you should be doing everything in your power to keep it that way. It's just too good.

The answer, I'm lazy. When I was sick, I focused on my mind with a desperate intensity. But as life got good, then great, I started to coast. Let the mind drift to its natural devices. Went days, then weeks without meditating. Loving myself became something I assumed, but didn't work towards.

I'm now at the point that when I repeat the loop, "I love myself," it feels strange. I find myself searching for a less powerful word. One that feels right.

But if love isn't right, nothing else will be.

The irony is, I'm the one who shared this truth with friends. "Love yourself," I told them, "see what it did for me. It works, it really works." All true. But who wants to take financial advice from a man barely scraping by?

So I ask myself the question, "if I loved myself, truly and deeply, what would I do?" I love this question. There is no threat, no right or wrong answer, only an invitation to my truth in this present moment.

The answer is simple: I'd commit to the practice. And I would also share the next thing I've learned, which is, don't let yourself coast when things are going great. It's easy to wish for health when you're sick. When you're doing well, you need just as much vigilance.

Honestly, it scares me a little. Coming from the dumps, when life works, it's great. But if life is working, and you do the practice, how high can life go? Can I handle it? Heck, do I even deserve it?

It's a nice trick the monkey mind plays. So I return to the question, "if I loved myself, truly and deeply, what would I do?" The answer comes easy: I'd fly. Fly as high as I possibly can. Then, I'd fly higher.

Now, if you'll excuse me, I'm going to go meditate.

Thought

If we are made of atoms and molecules, and they in turn from smaller particles which are empty space and energy, then what are we?

Are we our thoughts?

Ever catch your mind in a mental loop, replaying some old story, an old hurt, the same pattern? Who are you? The thought or the observer of the thought?

If you're the observer, then what is the thought?

Or are you a thought observing another thought?

Perhaps we're just biochemical storms within synaptic connections in a brain that evolved over millions of years. Or maybe there is an observer, a deeper self. No proof either way.

I'm fine with not knowing. I enjoy thinking about it, but mainly to remind myself that ultimately, everything is theory. I care about what works. What creates magic in my life.

This I know: the mind, left to itself, repeats the same stories, the same loops. Mostly ones that don't serve us. So what's practical, what's transformative, is to consciously choose a thought. Then practice it again and again. With emotion, with feeling, with acceptance.

Lay down the synaptic pathways until the mind starts playing it automatically. Do this with enough intensity over time and the mind will have no choice. That's how it operates. Where do you think your original loops came from?

The goal, if there is one, is to practice until the thought you chose becomes the primary loop. Until it becomes the filter through which you view life. Then practice some more.

Sounds like work. Perhaps. But the nature of mind is thought. Choose one that transforms you, makes your life zing. The one I found, "I love myself," is the most powerful one I know. You might discover another. Regardless, please do it.

It is worth it.

Magic

I finish at the gym, walk outside, and sit on a wall by the driveway. Indian summer evening in San Francisco. Breezy, cool, fog above downtown. Delicious.

I love my life, I find myself thinking, I love my life, I love my life, I love my life. The thought flows as naturally as the wind. I watch the skyline – people ask why I let my long hair fall in front of my eyes…it's for moments like these, when I watch the world through wisps of silver – I love my life, I love my life.

Clouds move above, the thought shifts: I love myself, I love myself, I love myself, I love myself. I'm smiling, then grinning. All I am, my hopes, dreams, desires, faults, strengths, everything – I. Love. Myself.

If you can reach this point, even if it's for a brief moment, it will transform you – I promise you that.

The key, at least for me, has been to let go. Let go of the ego, let go of attachments, let go of who I think I should be, who others think I should be. And as I do that, the real me emerges, far far better than the Kamal I projected to the world. There is a strength in this vulnerability that cannot be described, only experienced.

Am I this way each moment? No. But I sure as heck am working on it.

Thousands of years ago, a Roman poet wrote, "I am a human being, therefore nothing human is foreign to me." I believe it to be true. So if this is possible for one human, it is possible for anyone. The path might be different, but the destination same.

Key is being open to loving ourselves. Once we do that, life casually takes care of the next steps.

Remain open to that one possibility and you'll experience the beauty of watching the world around you dance its dance while inside, you fully accept this marvelous amazing human being you are. The feeling is, for lack of a better word, magic.

Surrender

I once asked a monk how he found peace.

"I say 'yes,'" he'd said. "To all that happens, I say 'yes.'"

Before I got sick, the last thing my Western mind wanted to say was "yes." I was obsessed with my business, with visions of selling it, making enough money to never work again. You can argue that obsession fuels innovation in our society. True, perhaps. But quite often, behind obsession is fear.

And there was plenty of fear. Fear of what people would think. Fear of letting employees and investors down. Fear of failing and what that would mean about me. I used the fear as energy, driving me forward, pushing to achieve, pushing to succeed, paying no attention to my body, to the present, and I paid the price.

Often, the price for not being present is pain.

Now, I understand what the monk meant. There is a surrender to what is, to the moment. Whenever I notice fear in my mind, instead of pushing it aside or using it as fuel, I say to myself, "it's ok." A gentle yes to myself. To the moment, to what the mind is feeling.

Often, that is enough to deflate the fear. From there, I shift to the truth of loving myself.

Knowing this, I realize that I still could have built a great company, had a beautiful relationship, managed my health, and reached out to my friend before she passed away and told her how much I loved her. I could have done all of this from a place of gentleness, a place of self—love.

But I can't erase the past, only learn from it. It's ok. Applying what I know makes the present and the future a beautiful place to be.

Belief

A side effect of loving myself fiercely was that it started to dislodge old patterns, thoughts and beliefs that I didn't even know existed. Whether having coffee with a friend or reading a book, I would have flashes of insight into myself. They were so clear. It was like my life was a deck of cards, each with a picture of situations I'd experienced, all falling down at me, flip flip flip, and the only thought was, "Oh my God, it all makes sense."

Here's one example. I've always known that growth is important to me. If I don't feel like I'm growing, I'm drifting, depressed. But what I didn't know, until the practice of self—love showed me, was my belief about growth: real growth comes through intense, difficult, and challenging situations.

Can you see how that would define the path of my life?

It was immediately obvious where it came from. The first time I felt like I grew in a way that I was no longer the same, I was far better: US Army Infantry bootcamp. Was it intense, yes. Was it difficult, yes. Was it challenging, every day. Was it happy or joyful, no way. Centuries of military protocol designed it to be miserable. But it's something I've always looked at as a defining experience, one I'm proud of. I went in as an insecure eighteen–year old. I came out knowing I could handle anything thrown at me. That was growth.

What we believe, that's what we seek, it's the filter we view our lives through. I've actively thrown myself at intense and difficult situations. All situations where I grew, but at what price?

Another example. In building my company, I came across as someone who was driven to succeed. Many told me so. I thought that as well until I loved myself. Then, one day, I woke up to a spotlight shining on that belief, except the truth was a slight twist: I was driven to not fail.

Huge difference. No wonder my company went the way it did. The intense and consistent work to keep moving it forward, one step away from disaster, always somehow pulling it off, then moving to avert the next disaster. Never failing, but never taking off the way I knew it should.

The good news is that once the spotlight shines from within yourself, there is no going back. The patterns of the mind that held you back fall away on their own. Like rusty old armor you don't need anymore. With each insight, there is freedom, a sense of lightness. And growth.

Oxygen

After I gave that talk at Renaissance Weekend, one person said to me, "you must love others first."

I respectfully disagree. It's like what they tell you during pre—flight instructions; in case of emergency, if oxygen masks drop from above, put yours on before you help someone else.

As I started to love myself, things inside me shifted. Fear strengthens the ego. Love softens it. I became more open, vulnerable. It was natural to be gentle with others, even when they weren't loving towards me. And the times it wasn't easy, I had the resources — the loop, the meditation, the question — to return to self—love.

There is a power in this. Rather than reacting to situations, I found myself choosing how I wanted to be. That, in turn, created better situations, and ultimately a far better life.

Where I want to be

Lying on my back on a hill, grass slightly tickling my neck. Beautiful sunny day, blue skies. Clouds drift above. Each, a thought. I watch, knowing them for what they are. Rather than attaching my experience of the present to them, I choose the ones I want to focus on. Or not focus on. Always my choice.

The thoughts come. Drifting, twisting, turning in shapes. It is their nature. I pick one for the moment, and then let it go, never attached. Simply experiencing what I choose. All through the filter of love. That's it.

End

This book could've been a cover, plus one almost–blank page with two words in the middle: Love yourself.

But if I had picked it up and read it, without knowing what I learned that summer, I wouldn't have applied it. At least not in a way that would transform my life. So, I've shared brief learnings, thoughts, and experiences. I could have filled it out more, but that only serves my ego. Rather, truth is simple. Truth is succinct.

I think that instead of reading loads of self–help books, attending various seminars, listening to different preachers, we should just pick one thing. Something that feels true for us. Then practice it fiercely.

Place our bet on it, then go all out. That's where magic happens. Where life blows away our expectations.

I found what to bet on. It came from a place of anguish, a place of "no more." But it doesn't have to be that way. It can come from a friend, a book, a lover. It can come from joy.

If something else feels true for you, then do that. I really don't think the details matter. What matters is the practice, the commitment to living your truth.

The results are worth it. I wish that for you.

Share

I wrote this book from the heart. To share something I learned, something that has been beautiful and transformative for me. Honestly, I was a little scared to do it. Putting myself out there like that.

But friends who applied the practice pushed me write it. If it wasn't for them, this book would not exist.

That is the beauty of learning, and then sharing. You grow. You share the lessons and help others grow. Here's the magic — they, in turn, make you grow. It's a natural cycle.

I hope you try out what I've shared here. It works.

If you would like to share it with others, you can send them the link below. It will list wherever the book is available.

www.founderzen.com/book

About the author

I've been fortunate enough to have some amazing experiences in my life so far. I've trekked to one of the highest base camps in the Himalayas, meditated with Tibetan monks in the Dalai Lama's monastery, earned my US Army Infantry patch, walked 550 miles across Spain, lived in Paris, been the only non−black, non−woman member of the Black Women's writers' group, written a novel, held the hands of dying patients, and worked with some of the best people in Silicon Valley.

But the most transformative experience has been the simple act of loving myself.

You can find me online here:

Twitter: @kamalravikant

Blog: founderzen.com

Please feel free to email me at k@founderzen.com

I'd be honored if you reviewed this book on Amazon. Thank you.